Lyrical & Pedestrian Preoccupations

Poems by Dave Roskos

Introduction by Tom Kryss

Art by Angela Mark, Loring Hughes, Michael Shores, Jen Dunford, and S. Clay Wilson

Cat in the Sun Books,
part of the reDUX Consortium
pubredux.com

First Edition.

Book cover by Angela Mark
& interior design by Kayla Riportella

ISBN-10: 0-9911523-8-7
ISBN-13: 978-0-9911523-8-4
Library of Congress Control Number:
2015957648

Cat in the Sun Books
5 Edgewood Road
Binghamton, NY 13903
Joe Weil, publisher
Emily Vogel, editor
Micah Towery, advisor

Special thanks to Ronald Nicolas Roskos, Jen Dunford, Matt Borkowski, Ken Greenley, Bob Surbrug, Joe Weil

The Anti-Civilization League, Michael Basinski, Bertha Sanchez Bello, John Bennett, Joel Bertin, Gene Bloom & Entrails-the magazine of Happy Obscenity

Thierry Bonnaire, Bree, Don Catena, David Aaron Clark, Jim Cohn, Cait Collins, Dave Cope, Rob Coulter, Michael Darrah, Edie Eustice, Charlie Ewen, Len Fulton, Ed Galing, Brother George, Andrew Gettler, Anthony George, Miriam Halliday-Borkowski, James Harbough, Skip Hoernig, Loring Hughes, Boni Joi, Dwyer Jones, Kathleen, Herr Klaus, Tom Kryss, Deborah LaVeglia, Maryellen Lebeda, Donald Lev, Misa Levey, Zakit Levine, Angela Mark, Jeff Maschi, Arthur Milgrom, Todd Moore, Tom Obrzut, Harvey Pekar, Michael Pingarron, Tom Pulhamus, John Lunar Richey, Bob Rixon, rjs, Kell Robertson, Scott Roskos, Stuart N. Ross, Kelly Ryan, Joe Salerno, Louis Schwarcz, Betsy Robin Schwartz, Pedro Angel Serrano, Michael Shores, Paul Sohar, Hal Stacey, Lamont Steptoe, Jerry Weido, Larry Weissenburger, S. Clay Wilson, Andrew Wingler,

& Micah, Kayla, Emily & everyone else at Cat in the Sun Books

These poems were written between 1983 & 2014. They are not sequenced here in the order they were written. Some of were published in the following publications:

Black Swan Review, Arbella, The Aquarian, Bouillabaisse, DIONYSOS (The Journal of Literature and Addiction), Drive-by Books, Flipside, Green Panda Press, Guts, Half Dozen of the Other, HEATHENzine, The Outlaw Bible of American Poetry, TOO MUCH Tales of Excess, (Unknown Press), The Energy of the Flesh (Iniquity Press), Intensive Care (Black Rabbit Press), Lyrical Grain, Doggerel Chaff & Pedestrian Preoccupations (Iniquity Press), JACK HAMMER (Beehive Press), Home Planet News, Temp Slave, Big Hammer, Street Value, Fall & All (Iniquity Press), LUMMOX Journal, Nerve Bundle Review, Poems of the Plague Fighters: Voices from the Needle-Exchange Milieu (NASEN), Lost & Found Times, Quimby, Long Shot, Cheap & Easy Magazine, Cokefish, New Jersey Bowel & Bladder Control, FUCK!, THE-HOLD Underbeat Journal #2, 48th Street Press Broadsides, The Mas Tequila Review, Barbaric Yawp, Working Hard for the Money (Bottom Dog Press), Blue Collar Review, RENEGADE FLOWERS: The LevyFest 2014 Anthology (Hydeout Press), Big Scream, Napalm Health Spa, Babel mag, COVER, Curare, Weird Poetry (American Living Press), The Paterson Literary Review, The National Alliance, Nerve Cowboy, Saint Vitus' Dance, Without Halos, Rubber Puppy & online at The Outlaw Poetry Network, POETS on the line, Babel, Napalm Health Spa / MAP (Museum of American Poetics), Busted Dharma, Misfit magazine, Concrete Meat Sheet, The The Poetry, The-Hold.

Thanks. Apologies to any pubs I couldn't recall...

Lyrical Grain, Doggerel Chaff, & Pedestrian Preoccupations

This book is for Ayler and Jen

CONTENTS

Lyrical Grain, Doggerel Chaff, & Pedestrian Preoccupations will remind you that everything -- waste paper emerging from melting snow in a lot, the memory of midnights in bus shelters at twenty below, tangled skeins of work places that read like a manual on how to survive without really suffocating, spectacles of solidarity with those who have nothing to give but themselves -- is, by far and away, worth our time and reflection. Accompany Roskos to, for instance, the Laundromat where on this particular occasion successive buffers of bad luck pinball him through so many twists and turns we almost lose sight of the equanimity of the human spirit and the humor that often informs moments of loss. Hunch down next to him in the shadow of the nacreous wall as he pulls the crushed pack from his coat and regards it with what amounts to a curious mixture of distaste and forbearance before looking you straight in the eye and asking the question he's asked so many times it's taken on air of guarded expectance, taps once, twice, allows your own hand to make the next move.

-- Tom Kryss

blessing & a curse
this poet business

maybe getcha laid
when you're young

hardly get ya paid
when yr work is done

the rimes are rolled
& the tales are spun

Ho Hum
on the bum

bowl of plums
gimme one

broke open a moon,
poured its milk
in the radiator.
hundred dollars worth
of gas
in two 50 gallon
tanks,
a cargo of constellations,
we put it in drive
& drove,
over state lines
& across borders,
gleefully giving
toll collectors
the last of our quarters,
paying for groceries
w/ broadsides
of out-of-print
Maxwell Bodenheim
poems,
lecturing state troopers
on the significance
of William Carlos Williams,
the importance
of needle exchange
programs

in the schools.
discussions about addiction,
its treatment
as a disease
& decriminalization
of narcotics
&, therefore, addicts.
where to end a poem
like this,
and how.

*

moonface tomorrow boned.
heartache painflower,
bent beneath the anvil hours.

flesh, forlorn & forgotten,
bliss born bloom begotten
in the milky marrow morn.

Dissonance is Bliss
Dissonance is Bliss
Dissonance is Bliss
Got a window to the future
& a heart clenched like a fist
Gonna pound today out of tomorrow
Hammer down sad sorrow
Dissonance is Bliss
Dissonance is Bliss
Dissonance is Bliss
Put your fingers
in the rainbow mouth
Bite down hard on your hand
Kneel down like Christ beside a camel
& draw a picture with your finger in the sand
Ride the camel to the moon's skull
Feed the flower to the fool inside of you
Dissonance is Bliss
Dissidence is Bliss
Dissonance is Bliss

Hallowed hollow moon
Eyeball full of swoon
Holy hungry halo heart

Should we ever fall apart;

another day to die in,
a different jig to saw thru --
ocean mouth asingin'

(a church mouse
turns a skeleton key
in my door
& leads a turnkey
through my halls)

a thousand tomorrows,
a hundred todays,
a handful of yesterdays
tilled & tossed
like dirt
on a coffin

no time for remorse!
kiss my eye
& ride my horse

Hallowed hollow moon
eyeball full of swoon
holy hungry halo heart
torn in two
 & blown apart

THE PRESIDENT'S PRAYER

Our fodder who art in cannon
Hollowed be thy blast
Thy shrapnel come
Our lives be done
On Earth where our bodies lie severed
Give us this day our daily rounds
& forgive us our near-misses
As we forgive those who near-miss us
And lead us not into active mine fields
But deliver us through evil
For thine is the ignorance
The powder
And the worry
Until Armageddon
ABOMB

I hadda
freight train
in my heart,
chugging thru
my aorta,
up & down
my arteries --
a cargo of sliver moons
& a few full ones;
all moon light
& no surprise.

i lit a candle
for my eyes.
i slit the throat
of a passerby.

i pulled a preacher by the hair
& led em down to hell,
we spiraled down a fiery stair
& upon our asses fell!

i burned a book of matches
& set a barn ablaze.
i felt just like a nothing mouse
trapped inside a maze.

I threw a hammer at the sun
& caught a hand grenade.
i bit the pin & tossed it back
& blew apart the railroad tracks.

**I stood on the river bank
& pissed on the moon's reflection**

in the end,
even words
are consumed
by fire.

the reflection
of the moon

a stream of piss
splashing in a river

a spider
frozen
in its web--

all for naught
& born to rot.

S. Clay Wilson

MASHED POTATO KISS CRUCIFIXION RAGA
an exhortation to the people

Crucify a Christ
mastermind a heist
rob a bank or two

Roll a rich man
kick a tin can
be bad, bad, bad.

Enter into sin
Fuck Fuck Fuck

Shit in the woods
like a bear
Declare that you
just don't care

Keep your planet
in your pocket
Steal some heirlooms
Hurry! Hock it!

mashed potato kiss
everlasting bliss

crazy gun
i almost cocked it
hidey-hidey-ho
i moshed it!

Dig like a dog
Crawl like cat
Hee Haw like a donkey
Bray like brat!

do wha diddy
clean your kiddy

put your pudding
in her pie
kiss her deep
make her cry

Twirl a world
on your finger baby,
stomp on a flower.

*

this is my message of hope:
succumb!
succumb, i say,
to the depths of nihilism
& despair
shake the wobbly warblies
from your hair
run & walk
& kill your stalkers
give ear
to the most ignorant
of talkers
hide & seek
& climb a tree
find a maiden
kiss her knee
breathe in the smell
of her hair

STUPID VISION

I swung from a gallows in my mind
felt my neck snap, my blood oozed
like sap from a severed tree.

I saw myself doing penance,
praying on my knees,
vomiting dope-stained rosaries.

I saw you from across the hall
there was an ocean or a river
between us & ghouls floated by
on desks feasting on
flesh cupcakes, bloody fingers
poking through chocolate icing.

I saw my best friend
and my dad
I saw selfishness
& everything I ever had

I wanted to share it with you
but you cut me with a razor
& hit me in the head
with a shoe

there was nothing left between us
so we left it on the floor
tore the door off its hinges
& shook it to its core

Blake wrote "Opposition is true
friendship," but then he crossed
it out, perhaps had some second
thoughts, as to what that was about.

God is an imaginary friend.
    policemen are just fiends.
        tomorrow is a cat in heat.

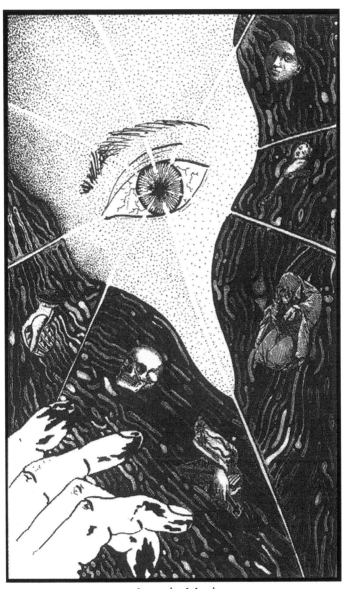

Angela Mark

HE BREAKS THE AIR WITH FARTS OF FIRE

He breaks the air with farts of fire
dances off rooftops, on telephone wires
magician of madness, orgasm sadness.
the television eyes of industry weep
sweet benediction. he can't believe
the lies his life has told him
& writes it off as fiction.
fleas hop on his pillow
cats crawl 'cross his bed
manuscripts & diaries weigh him down
like lead. kaleidoscopes &
ferris wheels. he breaks the air
with farts of fire, breathes in
deep oceans of mutual desire,
hasn't a home or pantry
or typewriting device
he smiles with his whole face
& tries to be nice.
the dawn is upon him,
motorcades of faith.
there's nothing left that's sacred,
his love's been forsaken.
sex is salvation
sweet kisses that salve
loneliness & heartbreak
the powder dissolves.

bar-room bathroom, a handful
of coke, "I wanna be sedated"
the words that he spoke
to a friend in a corner
lending an ear.
swing sets & slides
pamphlets & beer.
I'm down on my poetry
don't like it so much
caterwaul crazies
live in the hutch
a rabbit named rooster
a wig with a rime
rhythm & madness
in beatific time.

*

toot toot
don't shoot.
broken hearts,
sweet farts.
promenade,
balustrade.
up & down
with the
shades.
I'm goin'
to Hades,
where are
the ladies?

a mouthful of money

we are taught early on
that money is dirty.
it has passed through
so many hands
& we don't know
where its been.
Don't put that penny
in your mouth!
seems to be a refrain
echoed by mothers
everywhere.
Children, it seems,
just love to put things
in their mouths.
Human beings are orally fixated.
Filthy lucre. Suicide luger.
cocks & clits. balls & tits.
We all long to suck on nipples.
a mouthful of titty,
some cash in the kitty.
Ah, life!
Romance & finance,
get it while ya can.

I Wear Out My Welcome Before I Arrive
after, and for, Villon

I wear out my welcome before I arrive,
a coat sleeve caught on the edge of a suicide.
a sliver of ice, a crescent moon,
thirty pieces of silver, an unfurnished room.
I wear out my welcome before I arrive,
it's a wonder, they say, that I'm still alive.

torture tree toenail, a pail full of lies.
crazy alley cat abandon, a plague worse than flies.
stars torn asunder, rain made of fire,
battle horns broken, a deaf-mute town crier,
hunger, homelessness, lust & desire.
I wear out my welcome before I arrive,
It's a miracle, I'm told, that I even survive.

Rooming House Hell

You have been condemned
to rooming house hell.
You will never own a home.
You will never have an apartment.
You will walk with the rats
& the roaches for the rest of your days,
which are numbered anyway.
Enjoy your stay.

heroin haiku
for William Wantling

five days out of the cooker
she was still a looker
retired hooker

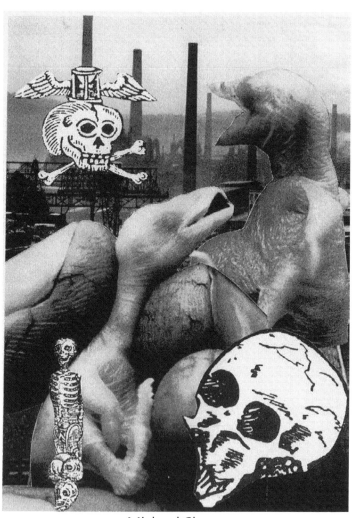

Michael Shores

SUICIDE BIRD

birds bash their brains
on the curb,
lift & smash their beaks
into the concrete,
stagger
& fall over
onto their bird backs
with their bird feet
in the air,
little X's on their eyes.
I shuffle through them
on my way out
in the morning,
kick them like tin cans,
their feathery bodies
flying through the air.

suicide birds
with bashed in brains
suicide birds
feel no pain

suicide bird
& i don't care
suicide bird
with mussed up hair

suicide bird
nada care in the world
suicide bird
impaled on a sword

Angela Mark

CERTAIN PROSTITUTE

she washed three valiums
down with a shot,
felt the need
to swallow my seed
& then to break
my heart.

I lie in bed
on the seventh day,
sink a soft needle
into the upturned
belly of my forearm,
taste sea salt
on my tongue.

I am in love with
a certain prostitute
who melts my love
in a spoon,
who leaves me empty
& as sparse
as the light
of a sliver moon.

a single mattress
on a paint-splattered floor,
cigarette butts
& the bitten off corners
of condom wrappers.

I followed a constellation
up the crack of her ass.

Summer

The moon is full of tears.
The sun is a dominatrix
with a barbed wire whip.

my eyes ache from lack of sleep,
scorched in the heat of day.

The city melts like mascara
on a transsexual whore,
a mixture of humidity & decay.

lunge toward motion

waiting on a train platform
underground
somewhere between loss
& longing.
Charlie Parker piped in
over the intercom,
voyeurs & oddities
in the shadows.
fingering the change
in my pocket
after a binge;
what have I done
& where have I been?
transit cops disguised
as janitors,
pushing dust brooms
& swishing mops.
bugs in a cigarette
& a lunge
toward motion.

a bit of a blank

it was business as usual
on a friday night.
Storm's dinner sat cold
& Mom paced the kitchen floor,
talking to herself,
rehearsing what she'd say to him
when he got home.
After us kids were finished eating
she'd wrap his plate in aluminum foil
& put it in the oven.
By eight o'clock
she'd be on the phone
with someone from Zapert's Lounge
asking if her husband was there,
being told, "no, haven't seen em
all night"
& placing the receiver down
sad
& lied to.
Outside in our sprawling backyard
we'd be yelling & playing
& jumping off the pump-house roof
onto the rope swing,
spinning each other around
in fast dizzying circles,
getting off

& staggering like drunks,
like our fathers,
wearily falling down on our asses
till our heads spun to a stop,
getting up & doing it again.

Around dusk Mom would call
my younger brothers & sisters inside
to wash up, get ready for bed & watch tv
& my friends & i would hightail it
outta there on our bicycles
before she got the chance
to ask me to do something helpful
like go to the store
for a gallon of milk.

Storm would usually get home
around 3 or 4 in the morning
if he came home at all
& Mom would ask him
for his paycheck
or what was left of it
because God damn it
there was no food in the house
& the electric was about to be shut off
& he wouldn't have much money left
& she would freak out & scream
& maybe punch him
& he would-- (its a bit of a blank--

*

one night i woke up
& Storm's car was
half way in the living room --
back wheels spinning
BLINKER/BRAKE-LIGHT
reflections
off shattered panes
of picture window glass.
5 cops trying to hold him down
as he thrashed back & forth
punching kicking screaming
THROWING them OFF.
i stood in my bedroom
& looked out the window
crying uncontrollably.
all the neighbors
standing in the street:
bubblegum machines
revolving red light
across their faces.

Body Bags Piled Six High on the Curb, Blood in the Gutter, Yellow Ribbons & Garbage Blowing in the Street

i can't remember anything
beyond blistered battered
brain blather burnt beyond
    the last evaporated traces
of some sullen summer's
    midnight morning snow
the radiant glow
    of blood on linoleum.

Storm punched out all the windows
in the French door--
small circles of bright blood
all over the floor,
smeared
& running down
the broken glass.

then he went after my Mom again
& Billy B. got outta bed
& tried to stop him
& Storm swung at him
& Billy reciprocated
& knocked a bunch
of his teeth out.

then we all, my Mom & us kids
& Billy & Karen & their daughter,
drove to Dunellen to hide out
at Billy's parent's house
for a few days
& i was happy
because i didn't have to
go to school that day
& excited because
i had heard about Dunellen
but never been there

he never let the cops
come into the house
with their guns.
he made them
take them out
of their holsters
& lock them in their cars.
because there were
children in the house
& there was no way
they were entering
his home armed.
he would reason
& scream
& insist
& the cops
would comply.

The Disintegration Dance
****

interstate 91 enroute to Glover
Vermont
no radio reception
just the sound of the car
cutting thru wind is enough
& the BLAST BOOM
of dynamite
decimating
painful memories--
eXpose yourself
eXpose everyone
Tell the truth
& SHINE OUT
all the darkness
Laugh & be merry
HA! HA! HA!
gonna die someday
>   green grass
>   lotsa trees
>   fresh air
>   hot flash breeze

Sometimes

Sometimes I forget what year it is
but I never forget the decade.
Sometimes I forget the state I'm in
& I'd like to forget the country.

Sometimes tulips talk to me.
when I wake up all I can recall
is their facial expressions;
their words recede on the horizon,
laughing like lilies on librium.

Sometimes, the doors & windows dance,
yell obscenities, crawl across
my mental floor, begging to be
beaten & slammed, just once more.

Sometimes, the blooms melt,
belt out a blistering caterwaul
of unholy terror that irks even me.
I shirk all responsibility & blow bubbles
with my spit, saliva dripping down my chin.

Sometimes, the bushes bleed daylight
& the morrow madness multiplies
a myriad pyramid eye, lensed like
a lacerated lily, lunging toward
elevator elbows of sanity.

Sometimes memories flood the face
furrowed; frozen in thought-moment
microsphere halo, car exhaust fumes
& children radiate light in a million
directions--lollygagged, lollipop abandon
mystery stick silent solitude kaleidoscope
handbag decoration device.

*

a coffee cup
can contain
an ocean.

an armpit,
an eternity.

In a place
that is
never quiet.
the pounding
of machines
hammering
substance
into salt,
water to oil,
bleach to wine.
correspondence
incomplete.
communication
discontinued.

you will search
these pages
for one good line.

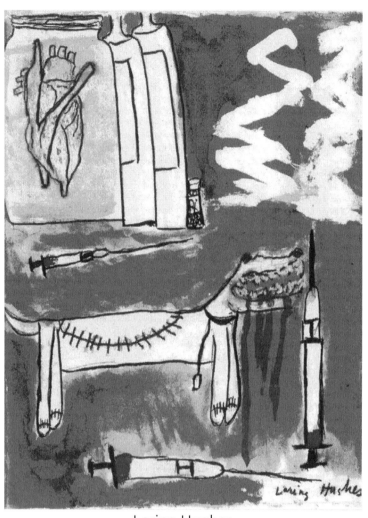

Loring Hughes

Dope fiends
of a future age
reading this
inebriated page
Know that in
a former time
drugs, sweet drugs,
were deemed
a crime!

Loring Hughes

junk dream

what we desire eludes us
what we can't set fire to
concludes us
pyrotechnic delight
don't put up a fight
surrender to the beast
inside you
this is sound advice
coming from someone
who knows,
speared like a lamb on a spit
charred & ready to
turn

locked outside of my
silly girl's love
locked outside of her loins
a lion rages
in my brain
waves a spike
that kills the pain

junk dreams melt
like powder & water
in a spoon
junk dreams dance
in the skull of the moon

junk dreams death
& they're dragging
the lake
junk dreams caw like a crow
& exclaim for Christ's sake!
curdle cream crow bar
broad-axe, bandoleer
I'm hanging like a monkey
in my junk dream
from a swinging chandelier.

THE JOINT OF NO RETURN

lit a joint at a party
puffed & passed it
never saw it again

it was the joint of no return

Garrison gunner
& a juggernaut spike
railroaded backwards
down Oblivion Pike.
nit-wit neanderthals dance
the ne'er-do-well waltz.
the dark streets of mourning call.
the parishioners file in,
church bells for brains,
dumb with pleasure,
numb to pain.
I threw up in a bucket,
resigned myself,
said fuck it.
wondered if I would ever write
a good poem
again.
Opiate Deluge.
morphine tablets sold
over the counter
in Paradise.
The resurrection of Free.

coffee pot toenail,
severed head on a stick.
what a lovely image
& a nice one to pick.
Out of all the visions
on the garbage heap
of desire,
I pull the ugly ones
out of the fire.

Loring Hughes

CRACKHEAD'S PRAYER

One last hit before my heart explodes,
God, one last hit.
Just let me get home
& cook up this bag
& I'll never get high again
(until next time).
Just grant that it's real, God,
that I didn't get ripped off
(again).
One hit, God.
One big blast.
One all encompassing,
aneurysm-inducing
heart attack of a hit.
One last hit before my heart explodes.
Just let me finish
this pile of rocks, God,
before you take me home
or the cops kick in the door.

Give me a little bit of that grace, Lord,

that you grant to us sinners,

us lost souls outside of your fold.

One last hit, God,

before the ticker

tocks its

toll.

coke smokers
& pawnbrokers
meet in the
midday glare.
once prized
possessions
await appraisal
upon a glass
counter top
& the coke smoker
does not care.
just wants to
pocket the cash
& get outta there,
to the cop spot
& to his hovel,
to cook & covet crack
& greedily grovel.
perhaps blow the ticker,
perhaps stop the brain.
the coke smoker
is the embodiment
of pain.

DEATH CALLS THE ADDICT HOME

Death calls the addict home
with promise of warmth
in an opiate womb.

safety in numbness.

an embryonic cocoon,
empty as the inside
of a hollowed out moon.

the fleece you wore
as protection against
death rays when you
walked thru dangerous
alley ways to score
doesn't fit you anymore

Poem for Paulie

the snow is so peaceful
when it's falling,
covers up the garbage.
I looked out the window
of the church after
the meeting last night
& thought of Paul B.,
Baretta.
He's dead due to a shot
he took in his arm
on a rooftop in New York.
He said he knew the needle
was infected, realized it
a second before he sunk it,
just had a gut feeling,
paused
& said FUCK IT.
He died in the VA Hospital
in full-blown dementia,
lesions on his skin,
pockmarked face--
snow settles on his grave.

Loring Hughes

Poem for What's-His-Name

this guy I usedta
shoot up with
had a box of alcohol
swabs, each individually
enclosed in its own
little paper packet,
just like the dope,
& whenever anyone
in the room got off
he'd rip one open
with his teeth
& say "here"
& we would
swab our respective
needle marks like
we were at the
doctor's office.

how's that for respectability?
health conscious junkies.
this guy was actually
very healthy, exercised,
ate right, held a job,
had a car & a place
to live.

one of the most responsible
junkies I have ever known,
and he does not have a name.

Poem for Scotty

I've known Scotty
a few years now.
We've both been
in & out of recovery,
in & out of the rooms,
in & out of active addiction,
in & out of The Grip.

When I came back this time
he was back 3 or 4 weeks
ahead of me & welcomed me back.
We'd bullshit a bit
before & after meetings,
talk about work,
lack of work,
Lou Reed
& The Velvet Underground.

I took his phone number
said I might be able to throw
some work his way
if I got any side jobs
moving furniture.
gave him my number,
asked him give me a call
if the mason he worked for

ever needed another
hod carrier.

He got a kick out of my business card:
Man with a Univan
& whenever we saw one another after that
he'd exclaim, Hey! It's the man with the univan!
famous in story & song!
& we'd both laugh.

The last time I saw him we talked for a minute
after the Sunday morning meeting.
I was depressed as ever,
my face a cross between
a frown and a scowl,
and Scotty came up
and slapped me on the back
and said Don't look so happy!

Coming from anyone else
this might've pissed me off,
but hearing it from Scotty
just made me naturally
break into a smile.
He had a very disarming sense of humor.

When I walked into the Sunday morning meeting
the day after Christmas, one week later,
the first thing I thought was Oh shit, who died?

A third of the people in the room were crying
and everyone else looked sad.

I took a seat and hoped it wasn't anyone I
knew.

We should all be so lucky.

Very few of us are.

His nine year old daughter found him
on the bathroom floor
with a needle in his arm.

Just like Tanya R., who was discovered
dead by her children on her bathroom floor
with a needle in her arm.

Of course, neither one of them wanted
to die.
It's just that sometimes
one last time
is
one last time.

the young woman
with the Chinese
character tattooed
to the back of her
neck says she's
grateful for these
meetings, that we are
all really cool
& that she's grateful
we're always here
for her despite
the fact that
she's always
in & out.
she says she's grateful
she only has
hepatitis C
& not HIV,
that she's really
trying to be good

because she knows
if she keeps getting high
she's gonna get real sick
& maybe even die

after the meeting
a kind soul
with over ten
years clean
points out to her
that she isn't bad
trying to get good,
she's sick
trying to get well
& she blushes
like a little girl
& says thank you

the infamous
& indigent
rise to the top
like freebased
cocaine;
the reflection
of the moon
in a bent back
spoon.
Oh, swoon!
& sweep.
Weep with
the rush--
HUSH!

Friday Night at the Crack House

This ain't a party.
It's a group suicide.
We all go way back,
used to be friends.
Used to simply smoke pot,
drink a few beers,
listen to music,
have conversations.
Now it's Gimme the pipe,
Make some more ashes.
shot gunning the contents
of our lungs through
cardboard paper towel tubes.
If we live through the night
we'll be broke all week.
too juked to speak.
crackhead freaks.

Loring Hughes

termites tear at my sanity
big fella with a blow-torch
smell of burnt hair
as crackheads cozy up
smoking toenail clippings
& a reporter researching
a human interest story OD's
& keels over on the toilet
I'd tell ya how it ends
but I don't want to spoil it.

The Poets Are Busy

The poets are busy
drinking themselves
to death

metering out their breath
in blurted drunken whispers
muttering about imagined injustices
vespering volcanic through tears
elegiac in front of the liquor store at 6
a.m.
the street lamps flickering out
the metal mesh doors rolling up
a pint bottle procession
passing across formica countertops
into coat pockets

if the poet had something to sell
he'd hock it

make a crack pipe
out of foil to parch
spent lips upon

get a grip
or be gone

Loring Hughes

Poem for Narcos

Does the narco
have compassion
for the sick junkie
coke fiend?
Does the narco care?
Does the narco
comprehend addiction,
the nature
of disease?

The sirens never stop
up & down my block.
The sickness that prevails
pounds your head like nails.
Ya wander around trying to cop,
the loneliness dissolves you.
Crack, cocaine, heroin or bust--
pretty soon your bones be dust.

(If Satan appeared & turned his cock to coke,
I'da cooked it up for crack to smoke!)

Stop tapping your veins,
addict, before they collapse.
Quit thinkin' about
the rushes & highs

lest you relapse
& get caught
in the throes
of the lows.

Because the narco does not care,
would just as soon pull you by your hair,
pound your fragile face with fists,
& lock you up in jail.

*

Flush
& broke
at the same
time.
no longer livin'
a nickle-dime
existence.
I have put down
the pipe
& joined the
resistance.

Midway in my life's journey
I awoke on a stainless steel gurney,
tore the IVs out,
left against medical advice.
Didn't get invited anywhere
anymore, not even to funerals.
Boiled my future
in a bent spoon
burnt with soot.

There is no climate control in Hell.

I will not be back here
asking for another chance.

The lights of understanding have gone out.
The line breaks
are broken.
The last words,
last rites,
spoken,
performed,
perfunctory,
with ritualistic familiarity
& ease.

the moon
is defunct
as an image
in poetry --

drained
of significance,

played.

oh moon,
swoon
in a spoon
at noon.

Moon!
full or
quartered.

Moon!
two of them
cupped in my
wife's brassiere.

Moon!
melted down
& shot up
by junkies.

(rubber gloved
dishwashers
with moons
in their
hair nets)

Moon!
halved or in
eigths
like marijuana
weighed
& bagged

to be
sold.

Moon!
lamented
& lost,
& at what
cost?

the whole
of the sky.

the chickens walk slow
in the yard around
the old rusted auto.

cautious chicken steps
taken lightly.

the rooster smiles
& the worms worry.

I, as an addict,
must stop
to pray.

On the Road to the Contagious Crack House

row houses
occupied by their original owners
first generation Hungarian
immigrants brought in
to the states by johnson
& johnson early in the
20th century

plaster Madonnas
& no shortage
of shrines

an occasional
goldfish pond
gone stagnant
with dis-
ease

4 foot high
chain link
fences

gates
off kilter
scratching
grooves into
the sidewalk --

& everything
leaning a little.

Cinquain For A New World

of Love.
Spiritual U-
nity. Nurture a Child's
Heart & Mind, in ourselves & our

Children.

Noon
with Ayler
at Manasquan Inlet

a clam boat
slowly approaching

Jersey shore towns
are ghost towns
in winter

a brief respite
from the tourists
of summer

boat in inlet now
raising its hoists

one lone worker on deck
in orange hip waders
spackle buckets
overflowing
with clams

the baby
crying in the
next room

my wife lifts
her shirt

unflaps
her maternity
bra

guides our son's
infant lips
to one of her
nipples

phone receiver
cocked between
ear & shoulder

as she laughs

talking with
a friend

After Kreymborg

Keep the marriage bed pure.

We have no marriage bed,
We sleep on a fold-out couch.

Keep it pure then.

Veterans

In the laundromat
lovers fold last night's linen
like tired soldiers
folding flags.

twilight

walking by little league
baseball diamond --
the ghost of a boy
who drowned in the river
hits a homerun.

Earth Day

convicts
picking up garbage
on the side of the road.

every day is Earth Day
on the chain gang.

Agnostic Prayer Meeting

"I'm going to start an agnostic prayer meeting.
Will you come?"

"I don't know."

After Ginsberg

Easter Sunday 1999
Dwyer & Loring just left
spent the night
watching movies, talking,
smoked a joint on the roof around
midnight.
read Allen Ginsberg aloud
from Cosmopolitan Greetings
    'After Lalon,' he advises:
"Allen Ginsberg warns you
 don't follow my path
        to extinction"
disillusioned with fame route
        he had taken,
honest enough to admit it,
so that others could learn
        from his mistakes.

Better to stay obscure?
move furniture for a living?
sweat of brow
& ache of back?

sore legs growing muscular
    through busy summer season
        trudging with dressers,
            boxes, sofas, appliances,
                pianos
Up
    &
        Down
            stairs,

On
    & off
        trucks?

maybe --
            more honest than
                teaching
& as seasonal.

work yr whole
life
w/ promise
of charred
meat

gristle
to gnaw
on in
yr old
age

flavorless
save for
the taste
of fire

empty 55 gallon drum
on its side
dirt splattered
after last night's rain,
bald tractor trailer tires
leaning on a 45 degree angle
against a green & white
aluminum tool shed,
also rain spattered.

a small pool of motor oil
seeping into the ground.

chunks of asphalt
scattered randomly
around the lot
& a 15 year old boy,
the owner's nephew,
picking them up
one by one & putting
them into a wheel
barrow, spilling
them in a pile
behind the shed.

our job doesn't start
for an hour.
the closing on the house
hasn't come through,
is delayed.

get a cup of coffee
& wait in the break room,
the dispatcher advises.

early morning talk shows
& aerobics on every channel:
GOOD MORNING AMERICA.

one of the drivers
comes in complaining
that the god damn
gears jam in his truck,
drops 55 cents in
the soda machine,
pulls the lever,
it's all gone--
he has to drink diet.
God damn it! he yells,
punching the machine,
I hate diet!

Don't punch the machine,
says the owner, sticking
his head in the door.
Keep the fucking thing full
& I won't have to,
says the driver.

met a would-be murder victim
on an elevator today.
his throat had been cut,
long fish hook scar
still scabby on his neck.
We were moving an old man
from Brooklyn to Lakewood NJ.
This young survivor
was getting the hell out of
Brooklyn, moving his stuff
in a cab to Staten Island.

"What the fuck happened?"
I asked him outside on the sidewalk.
"You wanna know what happened?
I'll tell ya what happened. I smoke
weed ya know, but I don't smoke that
nasty shit. I smoke hydro. These three
guys busted into my apartment & pistol
whipped me. I had to kill one of them.

92

I cut off his fucking ear. I had a big stash
bro, they thought I was a punk & they
could hold me up…"

His cell phone rang & he answered it,
half in English, half in some other language.

"Are you Portuguese?"   I asked.

"No, I'm Russian, a Russian Jew…
another Russian Jew did this to me."

"Oh yeah? I'm Russian too,"   I said, "Well,
half Russian. My grandparents left Yugoslavia
& Czechoslovakia in 1917 & settled in
Paterson."

"Paterson's a rough town,"   he said.

"Yeah, I know…they moved there in 1917
when the Revolution went down."

"Yeah," he laughed," a lot of people
got the hell out of there in 1917."

Damn, I thought, don't even know
my own language...

He had been in America 11 years.
His Mom stood a few feet away next to
his stuff on the sidewalk.
She looked very very sad
& worried, like only a mother can.

.

why he got canned from the poem factory
for Donald Lev & Tom Obrzut

Got fired at the Poetry Factory.
My poems were malfunctioning, they said.
Poetry Boss shook his head,
"There goes another one
who'll never be famous
till after he's dead."

    *

some developers
tore down the historic
Red Lion Inn

now there is a Walgreens
right across the street
from a Rite Aid

the workers look
like pirates
mixing cement
beneath oak trees,
carrying block in the sun.
building an addition
onto a home
the likes of which
they will never
live in.

"the movers are here"

still drunk from last night
        "sorry we're late..."

"where do you want
this aeroplane?"

"put it over by
the cement mixer."

"God damn!
You see that
Master Bedroom?
You can fit
my whole apartment
in the closet."

"What's this guy
do for a living?"

"he's an investment banker."

in the back
of a pickup truck
winding through
the backwoods of Princeton
with the other hod-carriers,
who, despite the fact that
they are from Guatemala,
are referred to as
"The Mexicans."
when speaking about
all of us collectively,
the boss calls us
laborers.
never mind hod-carrier
or apprentice --
most of these masons
don't even know
what a hod
is.
A hod is a
bucket or trough
with a long handle
that was used for
hoisting cement & bricks.

a hod carrier
is a mason's helper,
someone who
carries block & brick
& mixes cement,
or "mud."

Sunday 5:15 a.m.
Ayler's asleep -
  I fell asleep around 11
last night.
          made chicken soup
in the crock pot. woke up half
    an hour ago, it was done.
ate some. picked out
    most of the bones.
          it's raining.
nice not to have to go
    to work today.
a bit broke, but things
    seem to work out,
the essential bills get paid,
    the immediate ones,
        one by one
usually at the last minute,
        but why worry?

        who cares about
        such working class
            concerns?

        (working people)

Why express them in poetry?

        What is poetry?

constant smell of burning rubber,
or paranoia?

vacuum line
fell off & landed on
the exhaust manifold
($50.00 to fix).

burning rubber
smell in cab
of truck.

oh fuck.

homework to do --
you're through.

The smell of burning rubber haunted him.

He was more concerned
with the mechanical condition
of his truck
than he was with
his own health,
took better care
of the truck,

& became a hypochondriac
in regards to
the truck.
always worried something
was wrong,
calling his mechanic
with all kinds of imaginary
symptoms.

this poem has a blown
valve cover gasket.

OVERTIME SUITE

I

I saw garbage gleaming in the sun
aluminum foil flattened into asphalt--
some worker's sandwich wrapper,
a permanent part of the parking lot.
½ moon, almost 2 a.m.
at work
overtime
cleaning up for the big event--
only time of year
new hires like me
w/o seniority
can get time & a ½.
not fueling buses tonight;
cleaning.
scrubbed down a bunch
of blue-painted steel doors
w/ spray can cleaner foam
& rags.
last couple hours
been picking up trash
in the parking lot
where the big event
is to be held.
co-worker Chris is driving

the industrial floor
cleaner/street sweeper
machine around looking busy.
the foreman's playing
solitaire on the computer
in the foreman's station.
& the crickets are
conversating.
you can see the orange
tip of Chris's cigarette
light up as he draws on it
whenever he drives by--
the sound of the
machine gets loud
as he approaches
& then faint
as he circles
to the other end
of the parking lot

II

Sunday is carbon monoxide night.
the mechanics turn on every bus
in the garage & let em run
for hours, to see if they idle,
I guess. after a while, you
can see the exhaust--
burns yr eyes.

III

Redemption through work.
Addicts w/ work ethics.
Artists w/ work ethics.
Addict & Artist as one--
synonymous
(often
enough)
Transcending addiction
through art.
ART-WORK.
ART-WORK-ETHIC.
Work it out,
up, around,
in.
like a cock in the cunt
of time.
ART-CRIME.
OFF-RIME.
Find the center
of gravity;
solar plexus pull.
write a poem on a bus
at work getting paid for it;
Ethical.
Sweat falling off
a worker's face,
push-broom oblivion.

solitude in yr thoughts.
a smile on pay day.
flirting w/ bank tellers.
passing notes.
plotting worker
revolution dreams
or at least a better
contract. Arbitration.
Day Dream Nation:
"I totaled another amp,
I'm calling in sick."
the real work
that it's impossible
to get paid for;
then again, I'm on
the clock now
as I write this,
hiding on an
air conditioned bus
3 something a.m.
in a Transit
garage in New
Jersey; overtime,
$16.20 an hour.
"cut-price poets"
Brecht on Broadway
Hart Crane haunting
the docks looking
for the ghost

of John Wieners
behind the State
Capitol.
taking notes.
documentation
of mundane
daily activity
& worker thoughts.
transcendence,
or just not thinking.
music in the
rumbling of an
engine, beauty
in the turning
of gears, fan-
belts & pulleys;
producing motion.
the getting to
& from
back & forth.
Everything
& everyone
must move.

**solidarity
or We Are All Brothers & Sisters
in One Big Union**

in the break room --

no one says
God Bless You
when you sneeze

it's strictly
Go fuck yourself
& fuck you too

why do you curse
so much in yr poetry?
that's not poetry,
it's profanity.

all those poets
you publish --
they sound like
they just got
out of an
insane asylum.

it's so depressing.

how much did
it cost you
to publish
this?

you're crazy!

450 degrees

put two potatoes in the oven tonite
& promptly forgot about them.
Kelly & I went to the Szechuan Gourmet
& right in the middle of my bowl
of hot & sour soup, I remembered.
"Oh shit!" I exclaimed, "I left the fucking
oven on with two potatoes in it.
I better call my house-mates
& ask them to shut it off
before the house burns down."
The one house-mate whose last name
I could remember was unlisted.
Fuck!
I ran back upstairs into the
restaurant (because the phone in the
restaurant didn't work)
& said, "Jim's unlisted.
Do you know Eddie's last name?"
"No," she said.
"Gimme your keys."

I walked hurriedly to the car
& revved it up.
I took the corners sharp & fast
& only ran one light.
I like driving small stick shifts real fast.

It has always been a fantasy of mine
to drive a get away car
& actually get away.

I parked the car & ran inside,
pulled the potatoes out of the oven
and switched it off.
They were done.
kind of soft & shrivelled up,
not as big as they had once been,
& certainly not as hard.
Phew
I had gotten there just in time.
I drove back to the restaurant
and finished my soup.
My entree had arrived,
chicken with cashew nuts,
late nite menu, only $4.65.
It must have been my lucky day
'cause the house didn't burn down
& my soup wasn't cold.
We've got to thank the Goddess
for the small things in life.
I looked across the table
at my future wife.
She had half a plate of steamed vegetables
in front of her (she's the healthy one
in the relationship).

"So, did the house burn down?"

"No, it didn't burn down," I said,

"It's still there."

THIS MACHINE IS BROKEN

Washing machine broke.
Brought the clothes
downtown to the laundromat.

There were so many whites
I decided to put them all into
one of them extra-large
washing machines.

Then I put the dark clothes
into two separate regular
size washing machines
& approached the change machine--
it was broken.

I decided to drive up Route 71
to another laundromat & use
their change machine.
Did not feel like
putting myself
through the
always frustrating
& sometimes humiliating
routine of asking
other human beings
for change.

Got back from my quarter run
& was about to drop 4 dollars worth
into the mother of all washing machines
when the attendant informed me
that the machine was broken.

I had already closed the door
& it wouldn't open,
was jammed
& the clothes
were locked inside.

The attendant
called the owner,
but no one answered.

I noticed that if I simply
unbolted one bolt,
I'd be able to get
the door open.

I asked the attendant
if she had a wrench.

Of course she didn't.

I walked up the street
toward the Acme to buy
an adjustable wrench,

stopping at a pay phone
to try to explain
to my wife
what had happened,
wondering how on earth
I was possibly going to
articulate such a thing.

"Why didn't they put an
out-of-order sign
on the God damned
thing?" she asked.

"I dunno."

"Fuckin' assholes should've
put a sign up."

"I know," I agreed.
"Is the chicken done?
How'd the rice come out?"

"The chickens done,
but I can't figure out
what's wrong with this rice.
I think you put too much water in it."

I explained to her how
to make the rice.
She asked a few more
questions & I said
"Look, I can't help ya
with the rice.
Just cook it till it's done.
I got enough to deal
with right now."
"All right, all right," she said,
"I'll see ya later."

"I love you."

"I love you too."

"Goodbye."

I had to piss real bad
the whole time this was going on
so I went into a Diner
& used their bathroom.
Then I walked to the Acme
to buy an adjustable wrench.
They didn't have any.

I walked back to the car
& drove to one of those
Super Shopping Centers

for the 21st Century Consumer.
They had adjustable wrenches,
but they cost eight bucks.
I bought one & drove back
to the laundromat.

I stood before the washing machine
tearing the adjustable wrench
out of its cardboard
& plastic packaging.

The attendant informed me
that she had gotten through
to the owner on the telephone
& that he didn't want me taking
his washing machine apart.

I could come back in the morning
& he would get my clothes
out of the washer for me.

Great, I thought, I just paid
eight bucks for this fuckin' wrench
for nothing.
Ah, well, fuck it, I conceded,
never hurts to own
an adjustable wrench.

I retrieved the dark clothes
out of the two regular size washing
machines & drove home.

The rice had come out fine.

"Anthony called while you were out.
He said he wants to do that poetry reading."

"Oh, good," I said,
"Is he home?"

"No," she answered,
"He had to go to
the laundromat."

TONGUE & GROOVE

home from work early
listening to Monk
& Sonny Rollins.
spent a few days
installing hardwood flooring.
back, knees, arms
ache.

have a bunch of poetry to read
have to either accept it
for publication
or reject it
& mail it back

but I'm so tired
& sore

think I'll sleep a while
first

installing hardwood floors
is kind of fun,
like putting a big puzzle
together

pays the electric bill too

so I can listen to Monk
while I write this poem
for you

MILES TO GO

listening to bitches brew
working on poems
it's not birth of the cool
or kind of blue
but it'll do

couple of the landlord's
employees
are cutting down a pine
tree in the backyard

always worries me
when he starts
doing work around
here

they are arguing now
about how to
take down
the tree

"the difference between you & me,"
the one says to the other,
"is that I know what I'm doing!"

sunday morning ¼ to 6
winter in new jersey

pity the poor flea market vendors
out here in the cold dark
desperate for a dollar
some living in their vehicles
selling junk out of broke down
winnebagos with bad timing belts

pickup trucks full of scrap metal
traffic tickets
for failure to make
repairs
asshole cops
administrators of hardship
a light dusting of snow
belongings under blue tarps
on wet asphalt

hard plastic nativity scene
duck-taped mouths
stopped up ears
cold feet
floppy shoes

stacks of records
floating atop
milk crates
of used clothing
& dishes

el gran combo
3 bucks each
good karma is to
take it or leave it
haggling begets more haggling
& does not always
have a place

cash money

ran into mickey
at the flea market.
he'd just sold a couple
old rusty trailer hitches
to the junk man
for five bucks.
said his girlfriend's pregnant
with a boy,
rattled off the unborn boy's name,
middle name of cash--
"after johnny cash?" i asked.
no, after cash money! he said,
rubbing his thumb & index
finger together,
cash money! my son is
never gonna pay taxes!
"yeah, i can dig it" i said,
"but i kinda like the
unemployment benefits
in the winter
when there's
no work..."

it was summertime
& winter was far
from mickey's mind.

RECORD GUY FLEA MARKET POEM

just listened to all six sides
of YESSONGS back to back
(much to Poet Girl's dismay).

recently got a mint copy
(with the poster)
in a new batch of dollar records.

can't see putting it in my dollar bins
for the cheap ingrates at the flea market.

I would be hard-pressed to get 2 bucks for it
out there.
they are morally opposed to paying more
than a dollar
for anything.

might as well keep it.

the record guys say they miss seeing me
at the market every week.
when will I be back again, they ask.
I'm here now, I answer.
Will you have more records? they ask.
I sure hope so, I say.

if they weren't so fucking cheap
I wouldn't have had to take a regular job
in the first place.

they love me so much
they put me out of business

anyhow, I have bought & sold YESSONGS
so many times, I figured I should listen to it.

I'm not that into progressive rock,
or PROG, as the record guys call it.

prefer fuzzed out 1960s psychedelic rock,
or PSYCH, as the record guys call it.
the musicianship of most prog bands
is just a little too refined for
my tastes.

very impressive triple LP.
can't deny that YES
were original & talented.
also can't deny
that Punk Rock
came just in time.

*

it was so hot at the flea market today
an ambulance came & rescued an old lady
who had fallen out from heat exhaustion

she layed on top of a weather beaten
plywood table amidst her secondhand wares
gasping for air till the medics arrived

the hospital and the ambulance company
have already sold her debt
to a collection agency

POEM WRITTEN WHILE LISTENING TO THE NEW MUSIC QUARTET PLAY ALBAN BERG'S STRING QUARTET OPUS #3

the dominion of dreams
darkens decadent doorknobs
dropping drearily down
upon the hate-hardened noggins
of demented carnival clowns
wringing dish water out of their frowns
in all night laundromats
in the city's heroin district

a volunteer army of
addicts

narco squad clashes with crackhead brigade

police retreat

crackheads resume occupation of tent city

demand decriminalization

PARKS AT RISK

dog walkers & buskers decry new ordinances

vandalism of surveillance cameras continues

mail-order heart attack
a crust of bread
super-glue shoe repair
muddy work boot abandon

the great not caring
reverberates above the
music of the machines

*

if all the bugs
dropped dead right now
the floor would need sweeping.

for all the celebrating
a fair share of weeping.

Narrow Apartment

Marissa lived
in a narrow
apartment

2 blocks from
Tompkin's
Square

the junkies nod on Charlie Parker Blvd.
cops beat ya on the head with a night-stick
for playing your alto without a permit.

Marissa lived
in a narrow
apartment

steel rubber bands
rapt round the neck
of her electric guitar

a journal entry for the urban gentry:
get the fuck off the hood of my car.

Blake's chimney sweeps are smoking crack in the
park
blatant in broad night day light can't wait till it gets
dark.

the cock suckers, too, ply their trade at all hours of
the day,
without permits or state funded routine medical
exams.

Coltrane coughed up blood on Marissa's living room
rug
she hung it out the window
of her narrow apartment,
was ticketed & issued a fine.

Dalachinsky is drunk
carving poems into a bench
on Charlie Parker Blvd.
Borkowski behind the wheel of a truck delivering
auto parts
planning his next drunk.

Meanwhile,
Marissa has moved out
of her narrow apartment
just 2 blocks from Bird Blvd
into an abandoned building
with plenty of width.

intent to share

a rutgers cop
handcuffed me to a bench

told me to contemplate
the error of my ways

busted with 3 joints
charged with resisting
arrest, possession,
& intent to share

he tossed my leather jacket
on a chair

oblivious
of the half ounce
hidden
in the lining.

Jen Dunford

WHERE WILL YOU SPEND ETERNITY?

Christian pamphlet
on a pile of papers
& dirty laundry
asks, Where will you
spend eternity?
It was given to me today
on 42nd Street.
I had just left
an adult bookstore
& was feeling
depressed.
I took it.
I always take them,
put them in my bag
or back pocket,
discover them
later
on the floor
of my room
in eternity.

if the shoe fits stick it up your ass

a "real book"
I want my poems
published in a real book,
the poet whined.
a real book
w/ a real spine
& a real cover
w/ a barcode
on the back
so it can be sold
in real bookstores

the poet blind
to the barcode
on his forehead

an mfa in creative writing
nothing to show for it
but debt

CITIZEN CONSUMER

Citizen Consumer
heard a rumor
Attorney General
took his rights away

Citizen Consumer
shrugged it off
He don't use his rights
anyway

The Moth of Destiny

The moth of destiny
dances round the light bulb
of desire; thinks it a fire.

the ceiling fan tills earth in my mind

morning.

two flies fuck
on the edge
of my coffee cup

tomatoes on the window sill
the vice president can't spell.
a wire-tap on every phone!
half the world without a home.
academics arguing,
you call that a poem?

GUN RACKS INTO BOOKSHELVES

the country slowly turned into a police state
& no one seemed to notice.

the world needs more poems
by single moms.

PLAYDROME

Jen & I
just played pool
at The Playdrome
for an hour.
we were the only ones
in the pool hall
from 4 to 5
on a snowy afternoon.
I used to hang out
at The Playdrome
when I was a teenager
in the late 1970s
& early 1980s.
it hasn't changed a bit
& I wondered if all
bowling alleys are time warps.
then we watched a group
of special needs adults bowl for a while
& I thought of my little sister Mary Beth
& how much she would
have loved Jen,
were she still
alive.

in the pediatric intensive care unit one day after Ayler's spinal fusion surgery

the boy is restless
despite the atavan
& morphine in his IV

he describes
his hallucinations
to me in detail.

he is having fun,
making the best
of a bad situation,
enjoying the benzo-
opiate cocktail.

might as well.

later on he wakes me up
startled

wants me to prop
a pillow behind his back

I'm driving a tank, he says,
I'm in a war-zone.
Hurry up!
People are depending
on me!

AMERICAN SPLENDOR IN THE GRASS

once when I was
talking with Harvey
on the phone
I asked him if he
ever thought about
writing a novel

he replied, No man!
I write comix!

I feel the same way
about poetry

II

another time
another phone call
he heard me coughing
asked if I was smoking
I said yeah
he asked what
I said tobacco
he said You should smoke pot
at least ya get something
out of it

Poem for Poet Girl

she appeared
in robes of rayon
commandeered the kissing booth
tossing valuable broadsides
& reality reefers
into the crowd--
money trampled
underfoot.

Angela Mark

THE PSYCHEDELIC EXPERIENCE

is the psychedelic
experience
distracting?

it can be unnerving
under less than
ideal circumstances

like a parking lot
full of cinder blocks
& police w/ riot gear.
bayonets & flowers
snakes curling
thru dollar signs
reflected in eyeballs
dilated pupils
pin-pointed by junk
the prophet is drunk
& doesn't want to
hear what's hidden
in pigeon chatter
mutter clutter.

Poem for Michael Pingarron

I hope death is not an ordeal
a swirl of bureaucracy
& paperwork
waiting rooms
& confrontations with clerks
in windowless cubicles

or is it a cocktail party
where everyone is young again
& doesn't have a drinking problem

Long live Michael Pingarron!

Captain Ahab
one wild eye
bent mouth
slurred speech
incendiary poems
spat like grenades
full of seeds

THE POETRY READING

he walks the walk
of a wounded man,
smokes his cigarette
with precision & grace,
unsure if it's his last one.
writes his last poem
before being sent
in front of a firing squad.
the wall he is standing
with his back to
is splattered
with stage blood
& bullet holes.
the lights come on,
everyone either goes home
or returns to their seats.
show's over.
fat lady choked
on a chicken
bone.

nympho number nine
couldn't read the signs
tell tale hearts
& used auto parts
a broken computer
that takes up an
entire room once
made the most unusual
sounds ever pressed
onto wax by a man
named Moe--
homicidal holographs
virtual manslaughter charges
1970s porno loops
projected onto a cinder
block wall during
a punk rock performance
an abortion in an elevator

Jen Dunford

daylight coming thru the blinds
early morning traffic sounds
vibrating the earth thru asphalt.
footsteps thru the ceiling:
people
running water
brewing coffee
taking showers
shooting up
starting their cars
punching in
punching out

a syringe full of thorns.
corona of charred crack pipes.
coat & tails made of
hundred dollar bills.
neon nipples.
third rail.

the state of Missouri
performed their last
public execution
in 1937.
It was a hanging.
vendors sold peanuts
to curious onlookers
& the hanged man
dropped.

AURORA BOREALIS

they call it The Ocean View
you can't see the ocean from there
what you can see is a multitude
of lighters firing up a multitude
of crack pipes
looks like the aurora borealis!
they be some bic flicking mother fuckers!
I don't even wanna talk about
what you can see in the daylight

EVICTION NOTICE

for Steve Richmond

grotesquerie on a rotisserie

severed head
on a revolving
pie plate

horse head stew

whatcha gonna do?

listen to gagaku

narcotize yer noggin'

eat the dead horse
you've been floggin'

mimeographed madness.
here a brief instant, then dust.
everything expires. funeral pyres.
the gyrations of a go go dancer
from when you were 23 years old
sitting in Billy's Topless, the way
a whore once took yr cock into
her mouth, simultaneously holding
out her hand for the money, the way
you fucked her face in that abandoned
telephone booth in the broke down
subway station, the crack dealers
paying no mind --
fear grindings
helicopter malfunctions
Baby New Year
& another dream drafted.
deferred dream explosions.
scissor man
& glue stick lady
rjs & d.a. levy
one writes letters
one doesn't.
        RANDOM is best --
the way things fall
                    & land.

the way the boss walks thru production
    all yeast & cock sucker suction.
FUCK FUNCTION --
            purple blooms on a branch
                    Easter Bunny fucking
                        Santa Claus in the ass

march 2 10:30 pm 06

Ash Ra Tempel on stereo
Renew Jerusalem by George Dowden
on coffee table.
bought the Dowden chapbook
at Antic Hay Books in Asbury Park
earlier today for ten bucks,
been reading it.
d.a. levy liked it.
shit & assholes
being the central
metaphor,
an asshole sun
shitting daylight,
dawn-dusk droppings.
Blazek published parts
of this poem in OLE,
levy published some of it
in the Marriwanna Quarterly--
it comes highly recommended

reminds me of Anthony George
          w/ the asshole visions...

                    fragments
               of skull
                    toes
          liver
                         lungs.
          bamboo torture--
     a tape recorder in a coffin.

the war then
the war now

the lives of poor boys
caught in red tape razor wire
disposable as shell casings

Circles

I go in them
They're under my eyes.

Jen Dunford

THE FIRST CHURCH OF JESUS CHRIST CONSUMER

jesus among
the olive trees

a long way from
cleveland

even farther
from home

passed the time
w/ some fishermen

built homes for
poor people

never owned
nothin'

said his poems
aloud

never bothered
to write them
down

only rich folks
had paper back then

there were no
mimeograph
machines

DOLLAR BILL BOOK MARK

television podium
porn shop nickelodeon
wastepaper trap
mouse fire
rodent strike

100 dollars for a signed
Douglas Blazek book,
purchased from
Allen DeLoach's
step daughter,
Heather.

front cover
& 3 illustrations
by R. Crumb,
3 collages
by d.a. levy.

lying in bed
reading it to
my girlfriend --

priceless.

ORIZABA!

I

the sea which
fed him his
livelihood
swallowed
him whole

foot caught
in the rigging
of the lobster
nets

overboard
like Hart Crane

ORIZABA!

II

Hat Crane
eaten by
sharks

poem-circled.

scent of blood
& bone --

not very lyrical.
not much music
in it.

A Memorable Fancy

bummed a cigarette
off Gregory Corso.
He was taken aback.
I said, "I'll give ya a poem for it."
He said, "Aww, now I gotta read yer poetry
too?"
I said, "No, it's by someone else..."
He said, "Oh, it's by someone else,
that's alright then."
Then he yelled across the auditorium to
Ginsberg
"Hey, Allen! Should I give this kid a cigarette?
Look how young he looks!"
Ginsberg glanced at him for a moment
with a perplexed look on his face,
then returned to what he was doing,
talking with a small gathering of
poetry enthusiasts.

earlier in the day
Anthony George & I
smoked a joint
with John Wieners
on the fire escape --
he was a little shot-out,
but read well.

I had heard him read
a few months earlier
at Jack Powers' Stone
Soup reading
series in Boston
& all I kept thinking
the whole time
is that a prophet
is not appreciated
in his home town

Peter Orlovsky Haiku

We once gave Peter Orlovsky a ride home
from The Painted Bride Arts Center in Philly
to his apartment on the Lower East Side.
I offered him the front seat.
He said, "No, that's alright, I like to sit in the back.
That way I can look out all the windows."

Jen Dunford

RESUME

a fortune cookie
recently promised
"a new economic opportunity"

a few days later
an old friend
called w/ news
of a job opening
at the non-profit
organization
she works for

I struggled with
writing a resume
for a few days
as the life
I have lived
does not fit
neatly
in the blanks,
is full of gaps.
large gaping gaps
that go on for years --

"& what were you doing
during this time period Mr. Roskos?"

Heroin.

"& this 3 year period in the early 1990s?"

Crack.

"You're just the applicant we've been looking for!
We can forgo the rest of the interview!
Let me show you to your new office."

SOCIAL WORKER

Poet Girl
said "don't call yourself
a social worker.
that'll really piss off
people who went to college
to be social workers."

someone else said
"Ya got a heart?
Ya give a shit?
Then you're a social worker."

Food Pantry Haiku

Don't have to go to the food pantry
anymore.

Got a job
bringing people to the food pantry.

Made in the USA
Columbia, SC
24 September 2022